Voices of Freedom

John F. Kennedy's Inaugural Speech

Karen Price Hossell

Heinemann
LIBRARY

Chicago, Illinois

© 2006 Heinemann Library
a division of Reed Elsevier, Inc.
Chicago, Illinois
Customer Service: 888-454-2279
Visit our website at www.heinemannlibrary.com

Printed and bound in Hong Kong, China by WKT Company Limited
10 09 08 07 06
10 9 8 7 6 5 4 3 2 1

Library of Congress Cataloging-in-Publication Data:
Price Hossell, Karen, 1957-
  John F. Kennedy's inaugural speech / Karen Price Hossell.
    p. cm. -- (Voices of freedom)
  Includes bibliographical references (p.   ) and index.
  ISBN 1-4034-6810-9 (hc) -- ISBN 1-4034-6815-X (pb)
  1. Kennedy, John F. (John Fitzgerald), 1917-1963--Inauguration, 1961--Juvenile literature. 2. Presidents--United States--Inaugural addresses--Juvenile literature. 3. Speeches, addresses, etc., American--Juvenile literature. 4. Kennedy, John F. (John Fitzgerald), 1917-1963--Juvenile literature. 5. Presidents--United States--Biography--Juvenile literature. 6. United States--Politics and government--1961-1963--Juvenile literature. 7. United States--Politics and government--1945-1989--Juvenile literature. I. Title. II. Series.
  F200.P75 2005
  973.922'092--dc22

                          2005006270

Acknowledgments
The publisher would like to thank the following for permission to reproduce photographs:
Corbis pp. title (Bettmann), 4 (James L. Amos), 6 (Kevin Fleming), 7 (Tony Arruza), 8 (Bettmann), 9 (Bettmann), 10 (Bettmann), 11 (H. Armstrong Roberts), 12 (Bettmann), 13 (Bettmann), 15 (Bettmann), 16 (Bettmann), 17 (Bradley Smith), 18 (Bettmann), 19 (Bettmann), 20 (Genevieve Naylor), 21, 22, 23 (Bettmann), 25 (Ted Streshinsky), 26 (Bettmann), 27 (Bettmann), 28 (Bettmann), 29 (Bettmann), 30 (Bettmann), 31, 32 (Bettmann), 33, 34 (Flip Schulke), 35 (Bettmann), 36 (Bradley Smith), 37 (Bettmann), 38(Bettmann), 39, 40 (Bettmann), 41 (Bettmann), 42 (Bettmann), 43 (Jack Fields), 44 (Gillian Darley/Edifice), 45 (Sygma/Bernard Annebicque); Heinemann Library p. 5 Jill Birschbach; Library of Congress pp. 14, 24.

Cover image of JFK reproduced with permission of Corbis (Ted Spiegel).

Every effort has been made to contact copyright holders of any material reproduced in this book. Any omissions will be rectified in subsequent printings if notice is given to the publisher

Some words are shown in bold, **like this**. You can find out what they mean by looking in the glossary.

Contents

Recording Important Events

One way to learn about what happened in the past is through documents written by people who were witnesses to history. Some of these documents are letters about events written by people who were there when the events occurred. Other kinds of important historical documents are written recollections of people who were in a war or **memoirs** of leaders after they have left office. Records of history such as these that can provide a firsthand account of an event are called primary sources. They are important because they tell us how people at the time viewed an event.

Other kinds of primary sources include newspapers, videos and sound and original drafts of speeches or other written documents.

Making sure these kinds of records remain in good condition is so important that they are kept in buildings that are specifically for that purpose. In the United States there are two buildings where many historical records are stored. These are the National Archives and Records Administration, or NARA, and the Library of Congress.

The National Archives and Records Administration (NARA)

The original documents in the NARA collection provide a history of the United States government. It houses paper documents and films, photographs, posters, sound and video recordings, and other types of government records. They also tell the story of American settlement, industry, and farming. In fact, documents and other **artifacts** detailing almost every aspect of American history can be found in the NARA collection.

Primary sources can be anything people wrote or created in the past.

Among the documents stored in the NARA is a group of documents called the Charters of Freedom. They include the United States Constitution, the Bill of Rights, and the Declaration of Independence. These historical records are on display in the public area of the NARA.

The Library of Congress

The Library of **Congress** is in Washington, D.C. It is a **federal** institution and also the largest library in the world. Its collection is available to members of Congress as well as to the rest of the American public. The Library of Congress holds about 120 million items, including maps, books, and photographs.

The Library of Congress is a popular tourist site in Washington, D.C.

Secondary Sources

Another category of sources are those written by people who have studied primary sources. These are called secondary sources. Scholars study these and write their own books and articles based on their research. When you write a research paper for school you are creating a secondary source. However, if in the future someone wants to study how students wrote research papers in the 21st Century, your paper could become a primary source.

The John F. Kennedy Presidential Library

Another place historical documents and other records are kept is presidential libraries. The presidential libraries are part of the National Archives. The libraries store historical materials related to the president and his term. The first presidential library to open belonged to Herbert Hoover (president 1929–1933). Every president since Hoover, except Richard Nixon (president 1969–1974), has had a library. Nixon's records are kept in the National Archives. Presidential libraries operate more like museums than like other public libraries.

On October 20, 1979, then President Jimmy Carter dedicated the John F. Kennedy Presidential Library in Boston, Massachusetts. The library is near where Kennedy's mother, Rose, lived as a girl. One of Kennedy's sailboats sits on the lawn of the library. Each year, about 200,000 people visit the John F. Kennedy Library.

The Kennedy Library stands along Dorchester Bay in Boston, Massachusetts. One of Kennedy's sailboats can be seen in front of the building.

Architect I.M. Pei designed the John F. Kennedy Library. It was completed in 1979.

More than 8 million pages and 6 million feet of videotape and film relating to Kennedy and his presidency are stored in the library. The records are important because they provide a firsthand account of Kennedy's life and his presidency. They are valuable references for scholars, students, historians, and writers. The same care is taken with these records as is taken with all of the materials at the National Archives. Among the many records of Kennedy's presidency is the original copy of Kennedy's **inauguration** address, which is kept at the library, along with a video recording of the speech.

United States Presidential Libraries

George H. W. Bush Library	College Station, Texas
James E. Carter Library	Atlanta, Georgia
William J. Clinton Presidential Library and Museum	Little Rock, Arkansas
Dwight D. Eisenhower Library	Abilene, Kansas
Gerald R. Ford Presidential Library and Museum	Ann Arbor, Michigan
Herbert Hoover Library	West Branch, Iowa
Lyndon B. Johnson Library	Austin, Texas
John F. Kennedy Library	Boston, Massachusetts
Ronald Reagan Library	Simi Valley, California
Franklin D. Roosevelt Library	Hyde Park, New York
Harry S Truman Library	Independence, Missouri

What Is the Kennedy Inaugural Address?

On a cold and snowy day in January, crowds gathered in Washington, D.C., for the **inauguration** of a new president. The year was 1961, and the president was John F. Kennedy. At 43, Kennedy was the youngest man ever to be elected president of the United States. For many Americans, his election—the first in the new decade of the 1960s—meant that a new day had dawned in American politics.

Kennedy represented many things to the people who had elected him president, including change, renewal, and equality. So the chill in the air did little to stop Kennedy's supporters from standing for hours in front of the United States Capitol to wait for the man they hoped would lead their nation into the 1960s.

This is the large crowd at John F. Kennedy's inauguration address.

The Kennedys leave the Capitol building shortly after Kennedy's oath of office.

President Kennedy, along with his Vice President Lyndon B. Johnson, wore a long, warm coat and a top hat to the inauguration. Before he got up to speak, Kennedy removed both. His voice was already a familiar one—millions had heard him speak on television during his presidential **campaign**. But on that cold day, as the microphone picked up his voice and carried it out to the crowd, they listened more closely than they ever had.

Kennedy had a distinctive Boston accent. People often made fun of or did impersonations of the way he spoke. But on this day no one cared about his accent. They wanted to hear Kennedy speak about what he planned to do in the next four years as the 35th president of the United States.

During and After World War II

The two decades before Kennedy's election had been very different from each other. In the first half of the 1940s, the United States joined other nations in fighting World War II. This war was fought primarily in Europe and the South Pacific. From 1941 until the war's end, Americans focused on supporting their troops and winning the war. They made great sacrifices for this cause. Sometimes the sacrifices were small, including donating metal items such as brass doorknobs, candlesticks, and pipes to be melted down and made into bullets or parts for ships. But sometimes their sacrifices were large. More than 400,000 Americans died in the war.

One of the many social changes that happened during World War II was that women began to work out of the home more frequently.

Life after war

It took awhile, but life began to get back to normal. In fact, for most people, it was better than before. Soldiers who had served in the war received free college educations. They often married and moved into small homes that were being built all over the country. The United States experienced what is called a "baby boom," meaning that more families were having babies than before.

As the 1950s approached, American life looked rosy. New jobs were created. New homes needed not only people to build them, but also people to paint them and people to make the paint. More homes had modern appliances and manufacturers sold hundreds of thousands of refrigerators, stoves, and ovens.

Television

Another new technology that became popular in the 1950s is still popular today. While televisions were first sold in 1939, it wasn't until the 1950s that ordinary people began buying televisions and watching them regularly. Families spent evenings sitting in their living rooms laughing at television stars such as Milton Berle or Lucille Ball. Kids gathered around the television to watch programs such as Howdy Doody. By the end of the 1950s, television had become an important tool not only for entertainment but also for politicians to make sure as many people as possible learned about their ideas for improving government.

This typical post-war scene shows a young family enjoying their television.

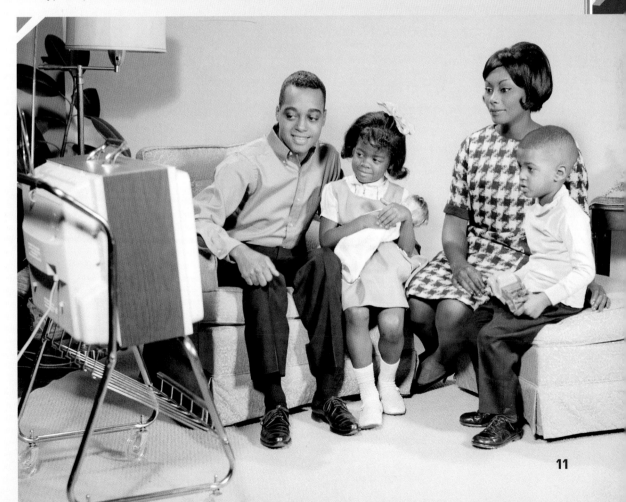

The Communist Threat

While the 1950s were good for many Americans, not all was rosy during that decade. In 1950 the United States entered into a war in Korea after troops from **communist** North Korea invaded non-communist South Korea. Thousands of Americans died in the fighting.

During World War II the United States and the Soviet Union had been **allies** against Germany. But, after World War II the fear of communism spreading resulted in another kind of war between what were at the time the two greatest powers in the world. The war was called the Cold War because there was little actual fighting and the two countries never cut off relationships.

The primary **debate** between the powers was how a nation should be governed. The Soviet Union believed in a communist government. The United States has always been a **democracy** and believed that was the best kind of government. The war went further than just differing ideas of government. Each power feared the other was so serious about spreading its ideas that it could attack at any time. For that reason, both the United States and the Soviet Union built up their supply of nuclear weapons.

A line of U.S. infantrymen march into the Naktong River region as Korean refugees leave.

Joseph McCarthy helped heighten fear of communism in the United States. Today the term McCarthyism is used to describe a series of unfair political attacks or accusations.

The bomb

The threat of the nuclear war put fear into the hearts of people all over the world. The United States had dropped a nuclear bomb on Japan at the end of World War II, which resulted in Japan's surrendering. Several kinds of nuclear bombs were further developed by scientists in the 1950s. These modern bombs had the potential to cause much more death and damage than any weapons previously known. Just the thought of one possibly being used caused terror. Americans built bomb shelters to make sure their families were safe, and schools conducted "duck and cover" drills that made people feel safe, but did nothing to protect students.

The McCarthy hearings

Senator Joseph McCarthy from Wisconsin helped heighten fear of communism in the 1950s by searching out Americans who had been communists in the past or who had associated with communists at one time. He brought many innocent people before Congress to be questioned about their loyalty to the United States, and as a result many careers were ruined. Kennedy and McCarthy were friends, but Kennedy did not agree with McCarthy's tactics and felt he went way too far with his accusations.

The Fight for Civil Rights

Communism and nuclear bombs were not all that caused unrest in the United States in the 1950s. Racism was also a major issue of the time.

In the 1950s African Americans suffered discrimination in all areas of life from work to marriage laws to healthcare. At the time **segregation** was legal, meaning that blacks and whites did not interact with each other. There were separate, inferior schools and hospitals for black people.

Brown v. Board of Education

In 1892 the **Supreme Court**, the highest court in the United States, ruled that African Americans could be forced to use separate public facilities if those facilities were equal to those whites used. In 1952 the United States Supreme Court first heard the case of *Brown vs. Board of Education*.

Segregation touched all aspects of life in the South.

Martin Luther King Jr. was one of the leaders of the civil rights movement.

In the court case, a young black girl was forced to attend a school that was far from her home. A school for white children was just down the road, but she had to board a bus and travel for miles to get to an all-black school. The National Association for the Advancement of Colored People (NAACP), decided to sue her local school board. The NAACP claimed this was not equal treatment because she had to go so far, while white students in her neighborhood walked only a few blocks to school. The Supreme Court agreed with the NAACP. They said that the child should not have to travel such a distance just because of the color of her skin. They changed the earlier court's decisions about segregation.

This decision meant that now African Americans had the right to go to the same schools whites attended if they wished. Brown vs. Board of Education only ruled that school segregation was unconstitutional. It would take years for other cases of segregation to be ruled illegal, but this case was the beginning of the end for legalized discrimination.

John F. Kennedy

John Fitzgerald Kennedy was born to Joseph P. Kennedy and Rose Kennedy in 1917. Joseph Kennedy was a bank president and would become the United States ambassador to Great Britain. Rose Kennedy's father served several terms as the mayor of Boston and later was elected to the United States House of Representatives.

In 1940 John Kennedy graduated from Harvard University. He then joined the Navy and went to the South Pacific. In 1943, two years after the United States entered World War II, Kennedy and other sailors were on a patrol torpedo (PT), boat when it was attacked by a Japanese ship and cut in half. Kennedy and his fellow sailors clung to the wreckage all night, then spotted land the next day and swam to it. Kennedy helped one injured man swim to shore. Later, he received a Navy and Marine Corps Medal for his heroism and a Purple Cross for being wounded in combat.

Political career

Joseph Kennedy was determined that at least one of his sons go into politics. He had hoped it would be his oldest son, Joseph P. Kennedy, Jr., but he was killed in World War II. John, or Jack, as he was called, was the next oldest. After the war Joseph Kennedy urged him to run for a political office. In 1946 Kennedy announced he was running for **Congress**. He won the election, and from 1947 to 1952, Kennedy

The Kennedy family in 1934. John Kennedy is the first boy on the left of the back row. Senator Edward Kennedy is the baby on his father's lap.

was the Democratic congressman from Massachusetts. While he was in Congress, Kennedy became interested in international politics, such as the building tension between North and South Vietnam. In 1952 Kennedy ran for a seat in the United States Senate and won. As a senator, he learned more about foreign affairs. In 1953 Kennedy married Jacqueline Bouvier, who was also from a wealthy family. Jacqueline Bouvier (known as Jackie) worked as a newspaper photographer.

Kennedy had badly injured his back during the PT boat incident in the war, and in 1954 and 1955 he had two back surgeries. As he recovered, he and his staff wrote a book called *Profiles in Courage*. In 1957 he won the Pulitzer Prize—an important award—for the book.

Running for president

In 1956 Kennedy decided he wanted to run for president in the 1960 election. Kennedy was Irish and Roman Catholic. At the time, no Catholic had ever been elected president. Kennedy was also young— if he won the election, he would be 43 when he became president. Many thought he would lose because of his religion and his youth.

The man Kennedy ran against was Richard M. Nixon. He had been the vice president under Dwight D. Eisenhower, who had been president since 1952. Eisenhower had a long and distinguished military career before he became president.

The New Frontier

Kennedy realized that Americans were ready to put World War II and the Korean War behind them. They were willing to begin to accept **integration** and welcomed many new technologies. Americans were beginning to look to the sky, too. The Soviet Union had already sent a man into space—the sooner an American could go into space, the better.

Kennedy's **campaign** platform included social **reforms** he thought were important to a new generation. His goals included a higher minimum wage, medical care for the elderly, increased **federal** aid for education, **legislation** for **civil rights**, improved life in cities, and major tax cuts. Kennedy also believed that the Cold War had gone on long enough and thought it could be "won" by spending more money on weapons.

Kennedy's ideas appealed to many Americans, but he was especially popular with young people, who saw him as a fresh voice. Kennedy had a friendly smile and a handsome face. He had a good sense of humor and enjoyed outdoor sports such as sailing and playing football. He had a beautiful young wife and a young daughter, Caroline, born in 1957.

Kennedy's youthful appearance and relaxed demeanor helped him do well in the televised debates with Richard Nixon.

Lyndon Johnson, shown here with his wife Lady Bird, was Kennedy's Vice President.

Televised debates

As part of the presidential campaign, Kennedy and Nixon agreed to do a series of **debates**. The debates would take place on both radio and television. These were the first presidential debates to be televised. Nixon was a more experienced politician. Many Americans believed he would win over the younger and less experienced Kennedy. But on television, Kennedy appeared calm and cool. He had an easygoing manner and a friendly smile, and he spoke well. Nixon, on the other hand, looked tired and appeared uncomfortable. He rarely smiled and had what is called a "five o'clock shadow," which means it looked like he hadn't shaved since that morning. The televised debates greatly helped Kennedy's campaign, and in November of 1960 he was elected the 35th president of the United States.

Know It!

President Kennedy chose Lyndon Baines Johnson (1908–1973), a former teacher and a senator from Texas, to be his Vice-President.

19

Writing the Inaugural Address

A newly elected American president takes office in January of the year after the election. The official ceremony that is held on the day the new president takes over is called the **inauguration**. Over the months between the election and his inauguration, Kennedy thought about what he wanted to say in his inauguration speech. He also discussed ideas for his speech with his advisers.

Three days before the inauguration Kennedy dictated some of the speech to his secretary, Evelyn Lincoln while they were flying from his family's home in Palm Beach, Florida, to Washington, D.C.

Polishing the speech

Kennedy worked hard on the speech because he wanted to make sure it reflected exactly what he wanted to say. He wanted the American people—and people in the rest of the world—to understand his vision of hope for America's future. He did not want to divide the nation by talking about Democrats and Republicans. One of his advisers, Theodore Sorenson, once said that Kennedy admired a famous speech by Abraham Lincoln called the Gettysburg Address and patterned his speech after that. Kennedy particularly liked how Lincoln used short phrases and simple words. Kennedy is said to have written and rewritten each sentence of his speech to make sure the language was as simple as it could be.

Kennedy often dictated speeches and correspondence to his secretary, Evelyn Lincoln.

Images like these of the young Kennedy family helped Americans feel closer to their president.

Even on the morning of the inauguration, Kennedy was concerned that the speech might need some changes. Almost as soon as he awoke on January 20, he asked Evelyn Lincoln to bring the speech to him, and he reviewed it. Historians are not sure if he made any changes to the speech that morning. When he delivered the 1,355-word speech later that day, he still referred to the yellow pages from a legal pad he had used to write the draft of the speech three days earlier. He did make some changes from the original text of the speech as he delivered it.

Inauguration Day

January 20, 1961, was a cold, snowy day. Kennedy's **inauguration** ceremony started at 12:21 p.m. and took place on the steps of the United States Capitol. A huge crowd watched the ceremony in person, and millions more watched it live on television.

The ceremony included prayers, the singing of the "Star-Spangled Banner," the reading of a poem, the swearing-in of both Lyndon B. Johnson and Kennedy, and the inauguration speech. The first person to speak was Roman Catholic Cardinal Cushing of Boston. As Cardinal Cushing spoke his prayer, he smelled smoke and opened his eyes to see a plume of blue smoke coming from the podium. The Secret Service men, who are charged with protecting the president and his family, rushed to the lectern and tried to be quiet as they searched for the source of the smoke. The Cardinal continued to pray but wondered if he would have to cut his prayer short to escape a fire. The Secret Service finally found the source of the smoke, which was in the motor that raised and lowered the podium to adjust to the height of the speaker behind it. They shut off the motor and the smoke disappeared.

John F. Kennedy is shown taking the oath of office from Chief Justice Earl Warren.

Next, an African-American opera singer named Marian Anderson sang the national anthem, "The Star-Spangled Banner." Then another prayer was offered by a Greek Orthodox Archbishop. Vice President Johnson was sworn in, and then poet Robert Frost stood up to read a poem titled "Dedication" that he had written especially for the inauguration. Frost placed the text of the poem on the lectern, but the sun was shining so brightly in his eyes that he could not read it. He remembered some of the lines, but he wanted to recite the entire poem or none of it. He quickly decided to recite a poem he had written years earlier called "The Gift Outright."

After Frost finished, Kennedy placed his hand on his family's Bible and was sworn in as president of the United States. Then it was time for him to give his speech. Even though it was freezing, Kennedy took off his coat and top hat before he spoke. After he finished what was one of the shortest inauguration speeches ever, a rabbi delivered the final prayer. A band then played "Hail to the Chief," which is the traditional song played when the United States President enters or leaves a ceremony. The new president, vice president, and their families and friends left the stage and got into waiting limousines, which would take them to a luncheon in the Capitol.

Robert Frost delivering "The Gift Outright."

Know It!

Poet Robert Frost wrote some of the United States's best-loved poems, including "Stopping by Woods on a Snowy Evening" and "The Road Not Taken."

The Speech Begins

John F. Kennedy's inauguration speech was short, but in it he addressed many ideas that were important to him and to the American people. First, he directly addressed the important people who were on the platform with him. In a formal speech, opening this way shows respect for those addressed.

Kennedy then spoke about the idea of the end of one era and the beginning of another. He said:

"… we observe today not a victory of party, but a celebration of freedom—symbolizing an end, as well as a beginning—signifying renewal, as well as change. For I have sworn before you and Almighty God the same solemn **oath** *our forebears* [ancestors] *prescribed* [ordered] *nearly a century and three quarters ago."*

The new era, he said, was one of renewal as well as one of change. The last line in this paragraph refers to the first time a United States president took the presidential oath—George Washington.

Next, Kennedy spoke about the idea that, through scientific discoveries, it should be possible to see that no one goes hungry or homeless. He referred to other scientific discoveries that resulted in nuclear weapons, giving people the power to destroy, all forms of human life. *"The world is very different now,"* he said. *"For man holds in his mortal hands the power to abolish* [end] *all forms of human poverty and all forms of human life."*

In his speech Kennedy made references to George Washington.

He then talked about the idea of human rights, saying:

"And yet the same revolutionary beliefs for which our forebears fought are still at issue around the globe—the belief that the rights of man come not from the generosity of the state, but from the hand of God.

The founders of the United States believed that the rights of man, such as the right to happiness and to freedom, come from God, and therefore should be guaranteed by the government."

In the next section Kennedy referred to Revolutionary War, which resulted in freedom for the United States. He went on to talk about a new generation of Americans who were born in the twentieth century and survived World War II. This generation, Kennedy said, will not allow the rights our founders fought for to be taken away.

"We dare not forget today that we are the heirs of that first revolution. Let the word go forth from this time and place, to friend and foe alike, that the torch has been passed to a new generation of Americans—born in this century, tempered by war, disciplined by a hard and bitter peace, proud of our ancient heritage—and unwilling to witness or permit the slow undoing of those human rights to which this Nation has always been committed, and to which we are committed today at home and around the world."

The possiblities of technology and science were themes in Kennedy's speech.

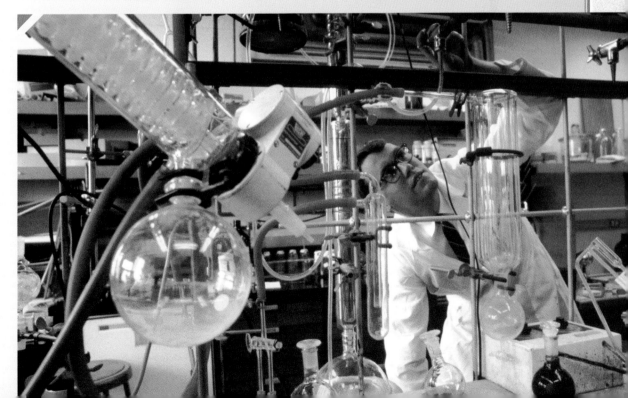

Working for Freedom

Kennedy said next that Americans will do anything to keep their country free. *Let every nation know, whether it wishes us well or ill, that we shall pay any price, bear any burden, meet any hardship, support any friend, oppose any foe, in order to assure the survival and the success of liberty.*

The next sentences refer to the **allies** of the United States. Kennedy said that we must continue to stand together for what is right.

To those old allies whose cultural and spiritual origins we share, we pledge the loyalty of faithful friends. United, there is little we cannot do in a host of cooperative ventures. Divided, there is little we can do—for we dare not meet a powerful challenge at odds and split asunder [apart].

After that, Kennedy mentioned new nations that had recently gained their freedom. He promised that the United States will always support them as they find a way to rule themselves. Then he warned that these regions should be careful not to replace a bad government with one that is even worse.

A few months after Kennedy delivered his inauguration speech, Soviet Premiere Nikita Krushchev unvelied this statue of Karl Marx (the founder of communism) in Moscow, Russia. The statue is located in front of the famous Bolshoi Theater.

The United Nations building is one of New York's best known landmarks.

Kennedy next promised those who lived in poor nations, who were trying to escape poverty or an **oppressive** government, that America would help them to be free. He referred to the **Communists**, who were trying to win over small countries by helping them or by invading them.

To those peoples in the huts and villages across the globe struggling to break the bonds of mass misery, we pledge our best efforts to help them help themselves, for whatever period is required—not because the Communists may be doing it, not because we seek their votes, but because it is right. If a free society cannot help the many who are poor, it cannot save the few who are rich.

As Kennedy continued, he said:

To that world assembly of sovereign states, the United Nations, our last best hope in an age where the instruments of war have far outpaced the instruments of peace, we renew our pledge of support—to prevent it from becoming merely a forum for invective [insults]—to strengthen its shield of the new and the weak—and to enlarge the area in which its writ may run.

The United Nations (UN) is a group of 189 nations whose goal it is to keep world peace. UN headquarters are in New York City. Kennedy was promising to support the UN as it worked toward peace in the world.

The Dark Powers of Destruction

In the next section Kennedy spoke of the "dark powers of destruction unleashed by science." He is referring to the nuclear bomb.

Finally, to those nations who would make themselves our adversary [enemy], we offer not a pledge but a request: that both sides begin anew the quest for peace, before the dark powers of destruction unleashed by science engulf all humanity in planned or accidental self-destruction.

Kennedy advised nations that consider themselves the enemy of the United States to begin a quest for peace instead of war. Next, he said that he believed that the best way to avoid war was to make sure the United States had more than enough weapons to fight any enemy:

We dare not tempt them with weakness. For only when our arms are sufficient beyond doubt can we be certain beyond doubt that they will never be employed.

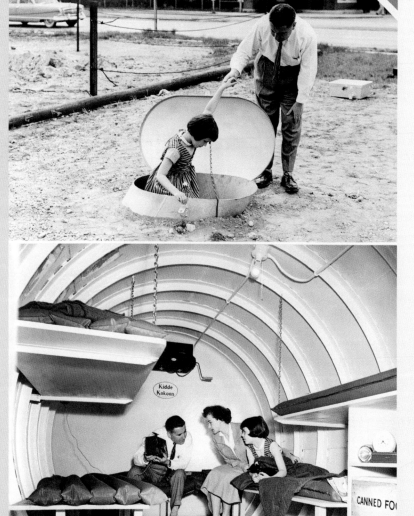

During the Cold War many Americans purchased bomb shelters to protect themselves in the event of a nuclear attack.

Then he went on to say:

> *But neither can two great and powerful groups of nations take comfort from our present course —both sides overburdened by the cost of modern weapons, both rightly alarmed by the steady spread of the deadly atom, yet both racing to alter that uncertain balance of terror that stays the hand of mankind's final war.*

Kennedy was speaking about the United States and the Soviet Union—both nations were stocking up on weapons to keep the peace because no nation would dare invade another that had so many weapons. But Kennedy believed that the cost of weapons made this an unsatisfactory solution to war. He again refers to the nuclear bomb when he says "the steady spread of the deadly atom."

Outgoing president, Dwight Eisenhower can be seen behind Kennedy.

Nuclear weapons

Nuclear weapons, or weapons of mass destruction, are powered by atomic energy rather than a chemical process. Nuclear weapons produce large explosions and dangerous after-effects. They can be delivered by plane, ship, or missile, and some are small enough to fit into a suitcase. The first atomic bomb was dropped on Japan by the United States during World War II. The first hydrogen, or h-bomb was detonated by the United States in 1952.

Working Together

In the paragraphs that followed, the president encouraged "both sides"—the United States and the Soviet Union—to work together to solve their problems. Next, he spoke about controlling arms, or weapons, to ensure that the world knows which nations have deadly weapons such as nuclear bombs.

So let us begin anew—remembering on both sides that civility is not a sign of weakness, and sincerity is always subject to proof. Let us never negotiate [work together to come up with a solution] out of fear. But let us never fear to negotiate.

Let both sides explore what problems unite us instead of belaboring those problems which divide us.

Let both sides, for the first time, formulate serious and precise proposals for the inspection and control of arms—and bring the absolute power to destroy other nations under the absolute control of all nations.

Next, Kennedy said science should be used for good, not evil. He then refers to the prophet Isaiah in the Old Testament of the Bible, saying oppressed people should be freed.

Let both sides seek to invoke the wonders of science instead of its terrors. Together let us explore the stars, conquer the deserts, eradicate [wipe out] disease, tap the ocean depths, and encourage the arts and commerce...

Soviet Premiere Nikita Krushchev, Kennedy's counterpart, was known for his animated way of speaking.

Kennedy started the U.S. Peace Corps to carry out his vision of helping people around the world.

Kennedy concluded by addressing the audience—his fellow citizens— putting on their shoulders the responsibility for taking on what he described above.

All this will not be finished in the first 100 days. Nor will it be finished in the first 1,000 days, nor in the life of this Administration, nor even perhaps in our lifetime on this planet. But let us begin.

In your hands, my fellow citizens, more than in mine, will rest the final success or failure of our course. Since this country was founded, each generation of Americans has been summoned to give testimony to its national loyalty. The graves of young Americans who answered the call to service surround the globe.

A Call to Action

In the next section, Kennedy uses a speech and writing technique called "parallel structure" to call Americans to action. In parallel structure, sentences with a similar pattern are repeated several times.

Now the trumpet summons us again—not as a call to bear arms, though arms we need; not as a call to battle, though embattled we are-but a call to bear the burden of a long twilight struggle, year in and year out, "rejoicing in hope, patient in tribulation"—a struggle against the common enemies of man: tyranny, poverty, disease, and war itself.

Can we forge against these enemies a grand and global alliance, North and South, East and West, that can assure a more fruitful life for all mankind? Will you join in that historic effort?

Next, he compared American's defense of freedom to a light that would spread around the world:

In the long history of the world, only a few generations have been granted the role of defending freedom in its hour of maximum danger. I do not shrink from this responsibility—I welcome it. I do not believe that any of us would exchange places with any other people or any other generation. The energy, the faith, the devotion which we bring to this endeavor [effort] will light our country and all who serve it-and the glow from that fire can truly light the world.

When Kennedy spoke of the light the United States would spread around the world he was echoing the words of Cotton Mather, a Puritan who spoke of America as a light for other nations.

John Kennedy and his son walk outside the White House.

The next paragraph contains the most well-known phrase of the speech:

> *And so, my fellow Americans: ask not what your country can do for you—ask what you can do for your country.*
>
> *My fellow citizens of the world: ask not what America will do for you, but what together we can do for the freedom of man.*

He then ends the speech by referring to the importance of doing God's work on earth.

> *Finally, whether you are citizens of America or citizens of the world, ask of us the same high standards of strength and sacrifice which we ask of you With a good conscience our only sure reward, with history the final judge of our deeds, let us go forth to lead the land we love, asking His blessing and His help, but knowing that here on earth God's work must truly be our own.*

One American's reaction

Steve Graw, a former Cornell University professor who was fourteen when he heard Kennedy's inauguration speech, later wrote that " ... the Kennedys symbolized what people wanted to be like, and they promised a nation that people wanted to have, a society that was still coming out of the haze of the repressive, anti-communist and Korean war times ... the inaugural speech eloquently gave people what they wanted to hear and followed up on what JFK had promised in the campaign. Sacrifice ("Share any burden"), service ("ask ... what you can do for your country"), and the goal of winning the Cold War and keeping the United States number one in the world."

Social Reform

Soon after he became president, Kennedy worked toward the goal of peace by forming the Peace Corps. Its goal was to promote peace and friendship among different people and nations. Peace Corps volunteers go to countries to help with education, healthcare, technology, or any area they are needed. To promote more understanding among countries, they learn how other people live and show those people how Americans live. The Peace Corps continues today.

Civil rights

Kennedy also turned his attention to the subject of **civil rights**. In the 1950s and 1960s, the Cold War had been such a concern for the United States government that it did not place great importance on civil rights. But Martin Luther King Jr. and his followers brought attention to the problems that were occurring as the result of **integration**. In some cities—especially in the South—there were riots as blacks and whites fought over what blacks should be allowed to do and where they should be allowed to go. In September 1963, the violence affected even young children when a church in Birmingham, Alabama, was bombed by racists. Four African American girls were killed.

Civil Rights protesters at the March on Washington in 1963.

The space program was an important part of U.S. policy in the 1960s.

Kennedy realized the need for new laws against **discrimination** and wrote **legislation** that focused on civil rights. The bill he wrote banned racial discrimination in public places, prohibited employers and labor unions from discriminating against employees because of race, and denied federal funds to **segregated** schools.

The space program

Kennedy was also very interested in the United States space program. The Soviet Union sent a man into space in 1961, winning for a while what was called the "space race." But Kennedy was determined that an American not only go into space but land on the moon. He encouraged Congress to vote for funding for the National Aeronautics and Space Administration, or NASA, which was the **federal** organization responsible for the space program.

Trouble in Cuba

During his presidency the small island nation of Cuba was a source of anxiety for Kennedy's government. Cuba's government had been taken over by Fidel Castro, a **communist dictator**, in 1959. The island was only 90 miles from Key West, Florida, and its communist government represented the very thing feared by many Americans in the middle of the twentieth century.

The Bay of Pigs invasion

In 1961 Cubans who had left Cuba planned to overthrow Castro. They had been trained to invade Cuba by the United States **Central Intelligence Agency** (CIA). The invasion is known as the Bay of Pigs invasion.

The invasion did not go as planned. Someone had warned Castro ahead of time. As the ships approached the Bay of Pigs, Cuban airplanes bombed them. The American boats wrecked on a coral reef. Once the invaders finally landed, a crowd of Cubans lined the beach to hold them until the Cuban army arrived. Over 1,000 of the 1,400 invaders were captured, and 114 died.

This street scene shows a peaceful Cuba during the Cold War.

Fidel Castro was a charismatic leader.

The Cuban missile crisis

The next year, Kennedy faced the Cuban missile crisis. The United States regularly sent spy planes over Cuba. One day in October 1962, as a plane flew over Cuba, the pilot saw missiles being set up and aimed at the United States. The pilot photographed the missile sites, and United States intelligence agencies studied the photographs. The agencies learned that the Soviet Union and Cuba were working together to set up the missiles.

Kennedy and his advisers met for hours to discuss what they should do. Some thought the United States should invade Cuba. Others thought the United States should drop bombs on the small nation. Finally, they decided to set up a naval blockade around Cuba, which meant that ships from the United States Navy would surround the island and stop any other ships from going in or coming out.

Kennedy then held discussions with the Soviet Union to settle the dispute. In November 1962 Kennedy agreed that the United States would not invade Cuba. He also agreed to withdraw United States missiles from Turkey, which was near the Soviet Union. Soviet leader Nikita Khrushchev then agreed to remove Soviet missiles from Cuba.

The Assassination

On November 22, 1963—1,037 days after he became president—Kennedy and his wife, Jackie, flew to Dallas where they planned to ride in a **motorcade** to a luncheon with local Democrats. The motorcade took them through part of downtown Dallas.

President Kennedy, minutes before he was shot and killed.

A man named Lee Harvey Oswald heard about Kennedy's visit. After studying the planned motorcade route, he took his rifle up to the sixth floor of a schoolbook warehouse called the Texas School Book Depository. There, he waited for the motorcade to drive by. As crowds cheered and waved at the president and first lady as their car passed by the warehouse, Oswald placed his rifle on the windowsill and pulled the trigger twice. One bullet hit Kennedy in the throat, the other in the head. Kennedy died a few hours later in a local hospital.

No one is sure why Oswald shot Kennedy, although people have come up with many ideas and **conspiracy theories**. Oswald was arrested in Dallas later the same day, and he said little about the **assassination**. The world never found out the truth or heard Oswald talk about the killing, because a few weeks after Oswald's arrest, a man named Jack Ruby stepped from a crowd and shot and killed him. Ruby claimed that he shot Oswald to punish him for killing Kennedy. Many people say that is not the real reason, and Oswald's murder only added to the number of conspiracy theories that came out of the assassination.

After Kennedy's death, Lyndon B. Johnson was sworn in as president. Soon after that, Jackie Kennedy accompanied her husband's body on a flight back to Washington, D.C. By that time, the news had spread around the world, and millions of people mourned the death of a man who was not only the youngest man to be elected president, but at 46 the youngest president to die.

Lee Harvey Oswald was assasinated shortly after his arrest.

Kennedy's family

Jackie Kennedy was 34 years old when her husband was killed. In 1968 she married Aristotle Onassis, a wealthy Greek businessman who died in 1975. Later she lived in New York City and worked as a book editor. For many people she remained a symbol of grace and glamor even after her death in 1994. Caroline Kennedy is a lawyer and is married to Edward Schlossberg. They have three children. John F. Kennedy Jr. became a lawyer and a magazine publisher. In 1999 he was killed in a plane crash along with his wife Carolyn Bessette and her sister, Lauren Bessette.

The Death of a Dream

The Kennedy era is often nicknamed "Camelot." Camelot was the name of the fictional kingdom of King Arthur and the Knights of the Round Table, an ancient legend. During Kennedy's presidency a musical about King Arthur, called *Camelot*, was popular. The name calls up images of a shiny, magical place where everything is hopeful.

Of course not everyone agreed with Kennedy's policies, or thought his presidency was wonderful, but even most of those who were against Kennedy's political views were shocked and saddened by his death. As news of his death spread, people all over America were glued to their televisions, watching as the story unfolded and trying to make sense of their president's tragic death. His funeral was held on November 25, 1963, and was televised all over the world. Kennedy was buried in Arlington National Cemetery in Arlington, Virginia.

The world grieves

Americans did not mourn alone. All over the world, people grieved over President Kennedy's death. Many world leaders attended the funeral or sent words of comfort to the Kennedy family and the American people. People in European cities held memorial services and placed wreaths of mourning in front of American embassies. Even in Russia, which was part of the Soviet Union and one of the enemies of the United States during the **Cold War**, radios played funeral music for hours.

Many stores closed in mourning for the unexpected death of the president.

Kennedy's funeral procession leaves the White House.

An unfulfilled presidency

During his brief presidency, Kennedy was not able to fulfill many of the goals stated in his **inaugural** address. One reason was that **Congress** was not ready to accept so many **reforms**. Another was that it usually takes a long time to get things done in government. Kennedy had worked hard to persuade Congress to accept his reforms. He had hoped to run for a second term as president so he could continue his work.

Know It!

In 1968 John F. Kennedy's younger brother, Robert, was a presidential candidate. While campaigning in Los Angeles, he was shot and killed. John Kennedy's only surviving brother, Edward (Teddy), has served as a senator from Massachusetts for many years.

Kennedy's Legacy

John F. Kennedy brought hope to a nation that had suffered through World War II in the 1940s and the Cold War in the 1950s. Many Americans saw him and his wife, Jackie, as what they wanted to be—young, beautiful, wealthy, and powerful.

Keeping the dream alive

Kennedy's ideas did not die when he did. Many Americans pledged to continue his work. So far, more than 168,000 people have served in the Peace Corps, which Kennedy established in 1961. Americans also supported the space program that Kennedy had encouraged. On July 20, 1969, two American astronauts—Neil Armstrong and "Buzz" Aldrin—were the first men to land on the moon.

Many people like to remember the glamorous years of the Kennedy presidency.

The Peace Corps is still active around the world today.

President Johnson continued Kennedy's work on a **civil rights** bill, and in 1964 **Congress** passed the Civil Rights Act. The act made **discrimination** against people because of race, color, religion, or national original illegal. Many of the strides made for equality and fair treatment in the United States can be traced to the Civil Rights Act.

After Kennedy's death, more young people became involved in politics. They protested when the United States entered into a war in Vietnam. They worked for peace and studied political science in college. Kennedy helped young people realize that they had a place in government and that they could make a difference in the world. Americans became more aware of discrimination and social injustice during Kennedy's presidency, and they carry forth his ideas even today.

Kennedy Memorials

Many people see Kennedy's assassination as the end of an era of hopefulness. The era that followed his death was difficult for many people. The next elected president, Richard Nixon, was impeached after it was discovered he had participated in illegal activities related to his election.

Because of this, many people remember the Kennedy era with fondness and many places have been named after John F. Kennedy to help people remember him. In New York City the Kennedy Center for the Performing Arts and Kennedy Airport are both named for him. In Florida part of Cape Canaveral, the location of the launch pads and other technical facilities of NASA, was renamed the Kennedy Space Center after his death.

Memorials to Kennedy can be found around the world. This one is located in Surrey, England.

Many American schools are named after Kennedy, as are numerous highways, hospitals, and libraries. The John F. Kennedy School of Government at Harvard University was named to honor one of its most famous graduates. Miami has the Kennedy Memorial Park on Biscayne Bay, which includes a memorial to Kennedy. A memorial in Daley Plaza in Dallas is close to where Kennedy's car was driving when he was **assassinated**.

Museum

Also in Dallas, the Schoolbook Depository where Lee Harvey Oswald shot Kennedy is now a museum featuring exhibits about Kennedy. Another Kennedy museum is in Hyannis, Massachusetts, near the Cape Cod complex of homes owned by the Kennedy family.

Overseas memorials

Kennedy memorials are in other parts of the world, too. In Berlin, Germany, a square is named after Kennedy. There are several memorials to Kennedy in Ireland, where Kennedy's family was originally from.

Kennedy's tomb in Arlington National Cemetary.

Glossary

allies countries that work together for a common purpose

assassination murder, especially of a political leader

Central Intelligence Agency (CIA) United States government agency that collects information about the activities of criminal and terrorist groups around the world

civil rights claims of personal liberty guaranteed to United States citizens by the Constitution and by acts of Congress

communist person or state that follows a class-free system in which land and industry are owned by the state; follower of communism

conspiracy theory idea of the possibility of a secret plot between two or more persons to achieve a particular goal

congress formal meeting of delegates for discussion and usually action on some question; lawmaking body of the United States government

debate argument that follows certain rules

democracy system of government in which leaders are elected by the people

dictator rule with absolute authority

discrimination unfair treatment of a person because of their race, religion, gender, or other reason

federal one central government that oversees smaller units; the smaller units, such as states, have their own governments

foreign policy plan for working with foreign countries

inauguration ceremony during which the United States president is officially sworn in

integration to bring people, things, or ideas together; racial integration is when people of all races mix together in schools, organizations, businesses, and neighborhoods

legislation laws made by the legislature

legislature group of elected individuals who make laws for those who elect them

memoir formal journal or diary

motorcade parade of cars transporting important persons

oath promise made in front of witnesses

oppressive denying freedom or other rights

platform plan of action to achieve a goal

reform official change from one policy to another, or any change in a policy

segregate separate or set apart by race or gender

Supreme Court highest court in the United States, consisting of a chief justice and eight associate justices

More Books to Read

Hossell, Karen Price. *The Assassination of John F. Kennedy: Death of the New Frontier*. Point of Impact Series. Chicago: Heinemann Library, 2003.

Kaplan, Howard S. *John F. Kennedy*. New York: DK Publishing, 2004.

Raatma, Lucia. *Profiles of the Presidents: John F. Kennedy*. Minneapolis: Compass Point Books, 2002.

Places to Visit

John Fitzgerald Kennedy Library
Columbia Point
Boston, MA 02125
(617) 514-1600 or (866) JFK-1960
www.jfklibrary.org

Index